D0330576

© 2002 by Barbour Publishing, Inc.

ISBN 1-58660-790-1

Cover image © PhotoDisc

Published by Barbour Books, an imprint of Barbour Publishing, Inc., P.O. Box 719, Uhrichsville, Ohio 44683, www.barbourbooks.com

ecpa Member of the
Evangelical Christian
Publishers Association

Printed in China.
5 4 3 2

GOD BLESS YOU,

Graduate

Ellyn Sanna

DayMaker
GREETING BOOKS

TODAY, AS YOU CELEBRATE YOUR GRADUATION,
PLEASE KNOW THAT I AM PRAYING FOR YOU.
I'M THANKING GOD FOR THE GIFT
HE'S GIVEN THE WORLD THROUGH YOU—
AND I'M ASKING HIM TO BLESS YOU,
TODAY AND ALWAYS.

AS YOU HEAD INTO THE FUTURE, MAY GOD HELP YOU TO. . .

* Use your gifts
* Live with integrity
* Do your best
* Be generous
* Believe in yourself
* Follow Him

THE LORD WILL GIVE YOU AN ABUNDANCE
OF GOOD THINGS. . . .
THE LORD WILL. . .
BLESS ALL THE WORK YOU DO.

DEUTERONOMY 28:11–12 NLT

One

USE YOUR GIFTS

REMEMBER the parable of the talents in the Gospels? In Jesus' story, the master gave farewell gifts to each of his three servants. Two of the servants made good use of those gifts, and by the time the master returned, the servants had far more to give back to him than they had received in the beginning. But the third servant was afraid to use the gift he'd been given. Instead, he dug a hole and hid it away where no one could ever see it.

When the master returned, he was proud of the first two servants—but the third servant's fear and lack of self-confidence earned him only his master's displeasure. The master said:

To those who use well what they are given,
even more will be given,
and they will have an abundance.

MATTHEW 25:29 NLT

8

DON'T be like that fearful servant. Don't hide your gifts in the dark. They'll do no one any good there, least of all yourself. Your own life will be poorer than it needs to be.

It doesn't matter how your gifts compare to those that others have been given. God just wants you to use whatever He's given you. And when you do, the world will be enriched.

Use what talent you possess:
the world would be very silent
if no birds sang there except those that sang best.

HENRY VAN DYKE

SOME people hide their gifts in holes—but others put their gifts up on the mantel to be admired like trophies. Either way, those gifts are little use to anyone.

We can take no credit for our gifts because they're gifts. God gave them to us through no effort of our own; we didn't do anything to earn them, any more than we earned our height or the color of our eyes.

And the best way to tell God *thank You* is to simply use what He's given us for His glory.

Make the least ado about your greatest gifts.
Be content to act, and leave the talking to others.

BALTASAR GRACIÁN

Two

LIVE WITH
INTEGRITY

OUR talents may be God's gifts to us, but our characters are our gifts back to God. We choose whether our character is one of integrity—or not. In a thousand daily, seemingly trivial choices, we shape the people we are.

If you want to be a person of integrity, then moment by moment, you must choose to live with integrity.

Good character. . .is not given to us.
We have to build it piece by piece—
by thought, choice, courage, and determination.

H. JACKSON BROWN

Take time to determine the way
you will live your life.
But once you know the way you should go,
let nothing distract you from your path.

Act quickly; think slowly.

Greek Proverb

13

WHEN you are right with God on the inside, that "rightness" will express itself on the outside. Living with integrity comes easily when it flows from your heart. Be true to God at the very core of your being. That commitment is like a seed that will grow and send out branches through your entire life.

And one day, those branches will bloom.

If a great thing can be done at all, it can be done easily.
But it is the kind of ease with which a tree blossoms
after long years of gathering strength.

JOHN RUSKIN

Conditions are never just right. People who delay action until all factors are favorable are the kind who do nothing.

WILLIAM FEATHER

THE ULTIMATE CAN ONLY BE EXPRESSED IN CONDUCT.
EXAMPLE MOVES THE WORLD MORE THAN DOCTRINE.

HENRY MILLER

*What lies behind us and what lies before us
are tiny matters compared to what lies within us.*

RALPH WALDO EMERSON

WORDS TO THE WISE. . .

* Ill-gotten gain has no lasting value, but right
  living can save your life.
* The LORD will not let the godly starve to death, but he refuses
  to satisfy the craving of the wicked.
* Lazy people are soon poor; hard workers get
  rich.
* The godly are showered with blessings. . . .
* The wise are glad to be instructed, but babbling fools fall flat on
  their faces.
* People with integrity have firm footing, but those who follow
  crooked paths will slip and fall.
* Hatred stirs up quarrels, but love covers all offenses.

* Wise people treasure knowledge, but the babbling of a fool invites trouble.
* The earnings of the godly enhance their lives, but evil people squander their money on sin.
* People who accept correction are on the pathway to life, but those who ignore it will lead others astray.
* To hide hatred is to be a liar; to slander is to be a fool.
* Don't talk too much, for it fosters sin. Be sensible and turn off the flow!
* The blessing of the LORD makes a person rich, and he adds no sorrow with it.

PROVERBS 10:2–4, 6, 8, 9, 12, 14, 16–19, 22 NLT

IN everything set them an example by doing what is good. In your teaching show integrity, seriousness and soundness of speech that cannot be condemned, so that those who oppose you may be ashamed because they have nothing bad to say. . . .

TITUS 2:7–8 NIV

Integrity means your life is based on truth. . .
justice. . .and right living.
Integrity means you have a conscience and listen to it.
Integrity defines the quality of your life.
Choose integrity and all its challenges.

VIOLA RUELKE GOMMER

Three

DO YOUR BEST

As you use the gifts God has given you,
as you live your life with integrity,
make up your mind to always do the best you can.

THESE three perspectives go hand in hand; you can't expect to do one while you let the other two slide.

You will not always succeed, no matter how hard you try. But leave the results of your efforts to God. Success and failure may look very different from His perspective than from your own. Put them both in His hands, and don't allow them to distract you.

Give life your best.

*I get quiet joy from the observation of anyone
who does his job well.*

WILLIAM FEATHER

LAZINESS MEANS MORE WORK IN THE LONG RUN.

C. S. LEWIS

*The roots of true achievement lie in the will to
become the best you can be.*

HAROLD TAYLOR

DO ALL THE GOOD YOU CAN
BY ALL THE MEANS YOU CAN
IN ALL THE WAYS YOU CAN
IN ALL THE PLACES YOU CAN
TO ALL THE PEOPLE YOU CAN
AS LONG AS EVER YOU CAN.

JOHN WESLEY

GOD BLESS YOU, *Graduate*

As you head into the new life that lies ahead, you will doubtless change in countless ways. New responsibilities will bring you greater strength; new freedoms will allow you to develop fresh aspects of yourself.

As your circumstances and environment change, you will adapt yourself in response. But you don't have to be passive as life shapes you. Instead, resolve to use each new phase in your life as an opportunity to grow.

God has called you to great things.

To change and to improve are two different things.

German Proverb

AIM HIGH.

SHOOT FOR THE STARS.

DON'T SETTLE FOR ANYTHING LESS THAN YOUR BEST.

Let him that would move the world
first move himself.

SOCRATES

Four

BE GENEROUS

THE DAYS THAT LIE AHEAD ARE FILLED WITH PROMISE.
GOD WILL SHOWER BLESSINGS ON YOU
IN WAYS YOU WOULD NEVER EXPECT.
DON'T FORGET TO SHARE THOSE BLESSINGS
WITH THOSE AROUND YOU.
YOU ARE NOT MEANT TO LIVE
YOUR LIFE ISOLATED FROM OTHERS.
ALLOW GOD'S BLESSINGS TO FLOW THROUGH YOU.
BE GENEROUS WITH ALL HE GIVES YOU.

If you give, you will get!
Your gift will return to you in full and overflowing
measure, pressed down, shaken together to make room
for more, and running over.

LUKE 6:38 TLB

LIVE TO SHED JOYS ON OTHERS.
THUS BEST SHALL YOUR OWN HAPPINESS
BE SECURED.

HENRY WARD BEECHER

Remember that when you leave this earth,
you can take nothing that you have received. . .
but only what you have given;
a full heart enriched by honest service,
love, sacrifice, and courage.

FRANCIS OF ASSISI

27

Don't store up treasures here on earth. . . .
Wherever your treasure is,
there your heart and thoughts will also be.

MATTHEW 6:19, 21 NLT

IN the years to come you will have the opportunity to accumulate many treasures: your own money. . .your own car. . .your own home. Enjoy these treasures, but hold them with open hands, remembering that God has only loaned them to you—and He means for you to share.

Your only treasures are those
which you carry in your heart.

DEMOPHILUS

Five

BELIEVE IN YOURSELF

SOMETIMES LIFE WILL SEEM TO SAY:
"YOU CAN NEVER DO IT."
"YOU'RE NOT GOOD ENOUGH."
"YOU'LL NEVER AMOUNT TO MUCH."
DON'T LISTEN
GOD HAS A PURPOSE FOR YOUR LIFE.
TRUST IN HIM—AND BELIEVE IN YOURSELF.

GOD BLESS YOU, *Graduate*

The beautiful is less what one sees than what one dreams.

BELGIAN PROVERB

KEEP AWAY FROM PEOPLE WHO TRY TO BELITTLE YOUR
AMBITIONS. SMALL PEOPLE ALWAYS DO THAT, BUT
THE REALLY GREAT MAKE YOU FEEL THAT YOU, TOO,
CAN BECOME GREAT.

MARK TWAIN

Insist on yourself; never imitate.
Your own gift you can present every moment with
the cumulative force of a whole life's cultivation;
but of the adopted talent of another,
you have only an extemporaneous half-expression.
That which each can do best none but
his Maker can teach him.

RALPH WALDO EMERSON

If a man does not keep pace with his companions,
perhaps it is because he hears a different drummer.
Let him step to the music he hears,
however measured or far away.

HENRY DAVID THOREAU

DON'T WORRY IF YOU CAN'T KEEP UP
WITH THE WORLD'S MUSIC.
LISTEN TO GOD'S SONG IN YOUR OWN HEART.
STAY IN STEP WITH ETERNITY.

Six

FOLLOW GOD

As you walk along the path before you,
it may seem strange and new.
You are not alone.
The one who made you
watches over you,
and guides your feet.
He knows the way.

VIOLA RUELKE GOMMER

LIVE WHOLEHEARTEDLY, BE SURPRISED,
GIVE THANKS AND PRAISE.
THEN YOU WILL DISCOVER
THE FULLNESS OF YOUR LIFE.

DAVID STEINDL-RAST

Your ears will hear a word behind you,
"This is the way, walk in it,"
whenever you turn to the right or to the left.

ISAIAH 30:21 NASB

FOLLOW GOD'S EXAMPLE IN EVERYTHING YOU DO. . . .
LIVE A LIFE FILLED WITH LOVE FOR OTHERS,
FOLLOWING THE EXAMPLE OF CHRIST.

EPHESIANS 5:1–2 NLT

Keep a clear eye toward life's end.
Do not forget your purpose and destiny as God's creature.
What you are in His sight is what you are
and nothing more.

FRANCIS OF ASSISI

DO THE JOB GOD HAS FOR YOU!

God wants to fit us perfectly in His plan,
if we allow Him to do so.
He is willing to bring all circumstances
to bear to that end.
Ephesians 2:10 tells us that God has already prepared, before the creation of
the world, the "good works"
that He wants us to do. . . .
He doesn't have to look around to see if He
can find a job to fit my qualifications
when I decide to apply to Him for employment!
No. All is prepared.

HELEN ROSEVEARE

ONE MAN WITH BELIEF IS EQUAL TO
A THOUSAND WITH ONLY INTERESTS.

JOHN STUART MILL

The remarkable truth is that our choices matter,
not just to us and our own destiny but,
amazingly, to God Himself and the universe He rules.

PHILIP YANCEY

*Take your everyday, ordinary life—your sleeping,
eating, going-to-work, and walking-around life—
and place it before God as an offering.
Embracing what God does for you is the best thing
you can do for him.*

ROMANS 12:1 THE MESSAGE

LET US BELIEVE THAT GOD IS IN ALL OUR SIMPLE
DEEDS AND LEARN TO FIND HIM THERE.

A. W. TOZER

GOD BLESS YOU, *Graduate*

ON THIS SPECIAL DAY OF PRIDE AND ACHIEVEMENT,
THIS IS MY PRAYER FOR YOU:

May the Lord bless you and protect you;
may the Lord's face be radiant with joy because of you;
may he be gracious to you, show you his favor,
and give you his peace.

NUMBERS 6:24–26 TLB